T0128724

No Legs to Walk but Wings to Fly

Hayde Navidad Watson

authorHOUSE®

AuthorHouse™
1663 Liberty Drive
Bloomington, IN 47403
www.authorhouse.com
Phone: 1 (800) 839-8640

Published by AuthorHouse   04/22/2016

ISBN: 978-1-5246-0230-7 (sc)
ISBN: 978-1-5246-0229-1 (e)

Library of Congress Control Number: 2016905638

Print information available on the last page.

Any people depicted in stock imagery provided by Thinkstock are models, and such images are being used for illustrative purposes only. Certain stock imagery © Thinkstock.

This book is printed on acid-free paper.

Chapter 1

My First Memories

My name is Hayde Navidad Watson. I was born Sunday, February 18, 1946, at midnight, in El Carrizal Sinaloa, Mexico. I would like to share a short story about my life with you. The life of a disabled woman, filled with love, family, friends, happiness, and hardships. My first memory was of waking one morning, at the age of two. The sun's beams were piercing through the cracks and holes in the one bedroom shack made of carton, mud, palm leaves, and dirt seeing poverty in its purest form. There only furniture was three cots with torn old blankets and small pillows filled with chicken feathers this was home. When I tried to get down from the cot, I could not move my legs I was paralyzed from the waist down. I was told later that I started walking at nine months old but contracted polio at the age of two, affecting my legs.

I was three years old when I first realized our poor living conditions. It was also during this time that my mom left my dad and moved us in with and left me with her father who was abusive to me from the beginning. He would abuse me physically and adding to that pain, he would verbally refer to me as "crippled, good-for-nothing, ugly, and no one will ever love you". These words stayed with me for a long time. Other family members did not properly care for me; they did not clothe, feed, nurture, educate, nor love me. At this young age, I was left to crawl around in the streets looking for food and water. I would ask the neighbors, who were also destitute could I wash their dishes for food. If they had no work or compassion for me, I would crawl to the mountain and eat fruit from the trees, such as mangos, bananas, plums, and other edible fruits that Mexico produced. I would drag myself to different locations across dirt, rocks, sand, thorns, hills, and slopes in search of food. Unable to reach the fruit on the trees or gather it from the ground, I would crawl to a memorial tomb dedicated to Malverde, a legendary man who stole from the rich to give to the poor. People would often light candles, pray, leaving flowers, and pesos as devoted offerings. Many people considered him a saint due to his generosity towards others. I would go there and take the pesos from underneath the candle wax to buy food such as tacos, burritos, bread, and water. I only did this on a few occasions when there was no food after being hungry for many days.

I learned at a young age that it was better to work or ask for money than to take it. My mother neglected all my needs. She would purchase nice clothes, cosmetic and top of the line hygiene products for herself. She did not bathe or wash me. I would go to the nearest water hole or pond and wash myself with rainwater. I had raggedy clothes, stained by dirt and mud that I would wash at the same pond that had green algae and lily pads with flowers on top. One day my mother came back to her father's house and took me with her because her father told her he no longer wanted me there. Forced to take me elsewhere, my mother and I took a train to Sonora, Mexico. We traveled by for three days, hungry and thirsty my mother failed to feed me; she showed me no kindness. A stranger noticed my situation and bought me two cheese and bean tacos and a small orange crush bottle drink. Once the train stopped, we got off and rode a bus to San Luis Rio Colorado, a border city of Arizona. We traveled for one additional day before reaching her half-sister's house.

Once again leaving me with strangers, my mother went to seek work in the United States as an illegal alien. She left early one morning without telling me she was leaving. The people she left me with did not care for me properly, often mistreating and rarely feeding me. I would go to the next-door neighbor's house asking for food when I was hungry they would feed me. One day my mother returned with a man and told me she was going to try to sneak me into the United States. We left, crossing the border passing through a fence and down a canal into the United States. I held on to the man for dear life from fear, as he carried me on his back through the canal. The man my mother hired to help sneak me into the United States continued carrying me as we traveled half the night through a field. That night we reached a small town in Arizona called Gadsden, where a car was waiting for us. We began driving to Yuma, Arizona when an old-fashioned looking police car, with a siren and lights, stopped us. It was the Immigration Department. One of the Immigration officers took me, along with my mother to the Immigration Detention Center and arrested the man that carried me.

The next morning my mother and I were escorted back to Mexico, where my mother left me with her half-sister's family while she returned to Arizona. The people she left me with attempted to sell me for one-hundred fifty American dollars, to a couple from the church who saw my poor condition and was interested in taking care of me. The day of the sale, they arrived late in the evening to pick me up to avoid being seen conducting the transaction. I was outside crying listening to the negotiations over selling me, and for the first time in my life I asked God "What now God? Where will I go and will they treat me good?" At that moment, a taxi pulled up, and it was my mother telling me, "let's go." Placing me in the taxi, she informed her half-sister she was taking me again. We went to the train station and headed to Sinaloa, Mexico. When we were on the train, I told my mother that the people she left me with sold me to that couple from the church and they were there to take me that night. My mom asked, "why didn't you tell me this earlier? I could have had half of the money and gotten rid of you at the same time" I felt her cold-heartedness unable to understand why she did not love me.

When the train reached a town called Culiacan, Mexico, we got off. She again left me with another side of the family; I was alone again with strangers. I was with them for three weeks before Nuns, from a Catholic convent, saw me, and showed sincere compassion for me. They asked me my name, and I said "Hayde". They told me they wanted to help me and teach me how to pray. I was four years old and became fond of the Nuns because of the kindness they showed me each time they came around. I woke one morning, and I heard the train whistle blowing and the people my mother left me with said "you hear that train whistle? Your mom is on that train, and you will never see her again because she left you for good". This family also mistreated and neglected to feed me so I would crawl outside looking for food. I came across two hen eggs in a chicken coop in the back, and I made a hole at each end of the egg and drank the yoke from both eggs. A family member caught me and he whipped me with a whip that they used to beat the burros. He whipped me so much that my back bled badly and later scabbed over; he hit my eye, leaving it blackened and swollen. Some of the kids saw it and ran to tell the Nuns that they were beating me.

The Nuns came to the house and found me beaten, bruised, scared, and alone.

The Nuns picked me up from the floor and said "come with us little girl we will take good care of you. You will have three meals a day and a place to rest, and we will make sure no one neglects or hurts you again". They seemed like angels, saving me from this horrible life I had come to know. They took me to the Catholic convent and school to care for me. My life completely changed there, I had a bed, plenty of food and shown love for the first time in my life. When they picked me up, I had head lice, was anemic, had boils, various skin infections, and paralyzed, from the waist down. My legs deformed from improperly healed breaks after falling from a burro, were in pain most of the time. It was so bad I would put my feet on my shoulders, back, and drag myself across the floor. After taking me to the convent, the Nuns started a donation fund to take care of all my medical needs. The Nuns would go to baseball games asking for donations from the people there. They raised three thousand pesos for my medical needs.

The recovery process began as they shaved my head bald because of lice. The Nuns treated all my wounds and fed me until I was healthy and strong. When I was healthy enough for surgery, the Nuns had the doctors perform surgical procedures to straighten my legs and bones placing metal pins in my hips, knees, and legs. I was in a half body cast from the waist down for three months. The Nuns would visit me while I was healing. They taught me basic verbal skills and words to help me speak clearer because I had a thick accent and did not pronounce the words clearly, but they were very patient with me and taught me well. The doctors placed braces on my legs after removing the cast and assisted me in taking my first steps. With the braces attached, to my wrist, I learned to walk again one-step at a time. When I healed enough to leave the hospital, the Nuns took me back to the Catholic school to teach me. There I learned discipline, respect, courtesy, kindness, faith, and love. I received a basic education learning to read and along with how to be a proper woman. The teachers at the school also taught me how to cook, sew, knit, make clothes, arts and crafts and how to defend myself. While at the convent, I met and made friends with other girls who were friendly and kind to me.

I started to work in the convent earning money, and purchasing items for my daily needs and I also began saving money for the day I was to leave as an adult. I also made crowns for funerals, piñatas for parties, and candles for various ceremonies. I maintained these jobs to the best of my ability always receiving compliments on my work. I was able to save five thousand pesos, which the Nuns kept for me until the day I left. At the age of fourteen, the Nuns offered me the opportunity to become a Nun but I declined because I wanted a life outside the convent. The Nuns contacted my mother, and they told her to come pick me up because they had done all they could for me, and I was ready to live life.

My mother sent her brother, Gilbert to pick me up from the convent. When he saw me, he was happy and pleased that I had healed from all my illnesses and had grown up to be a sweet girl. He then took me to see different family members to show them that I had not died on the streets. Some family members were pleased, and some were still cruel and unpleasant. Then we rode the bus for three days across the Mexican desert to Sonora San Luis Rio Colorado; the journey was scorching, but I would begin my new life in the United States. My uncle was very helpful and kind to me. I had a head full of dreams of a new and exciting life and hopes and expectations that things would be different. We went to the property that my mother had purchased for a hundred and fifty dollars. The house on the property that I was supposed to live in was a one-bedroom shack made of adobe and carton. When I saw the place, my heart sunk with the thought that nothing had changed, but I knew that I was going to make this place better and more presentable.

A week after I arrived, my mother came with a nine-month-old baby boy and an American man. I thought she was going to show me some love or affection, but she did not even greet me. When she introduced me to her new husband, she told him I was her niece and not her daughter. I felt very sad that she was ashamed to tell her husband who I was. A week later my mother's baby boy got sick, and the doctor said he needed a blood transfusion to continue to live. I donated my blood for the baby because my blood type was the only kind that matched. The Arizona newspaper published an article about a disabled girl who saved her little brother with a blood transfusion. My mother's husband found out who I was from the article. He took the news badly and told my mother he wanted a divorce because he found out she abandoned and disowned me at a young age. He could not believe that a woman was capable of such cold-heartedness and cruelty toward a poor disabled little girl. After that, my mother always blamed me for her husband leaving her. Soon afterward, my mother left her baby boy with me so I could take care of him while she worked. I became a mother at the age of fourteen.

She had me raise him until he was seven years old, and she would only give us fifteen dollars a month to survive. My uncle and I started to work at night making adobe bricks to sell. During that time, people were building houses, so we had many customers, and business was good. I made 10,000 pesos in a few days, which was a lot of money in those days. I started making so much money that I began to repair and rebuild the one bedroom shack. I purchased a stove, refrigerator, television, kitchen table, six chairs and a cooler for air conditioning because it was hot. I laid a concrete floor inside the shack over the dirt floor and then put tile. I later paid a friend to build four extra rooms onto the one bedroom building, making it a four-bedroom house. I put up new walls, replaced the roof, cut out windows, added a bathroom, kitchen, and laid rugs in the other rooms. I had electricity installed; light fixtures and electric plugs and I purchased lovely furniture. The shack transformed into a new house.

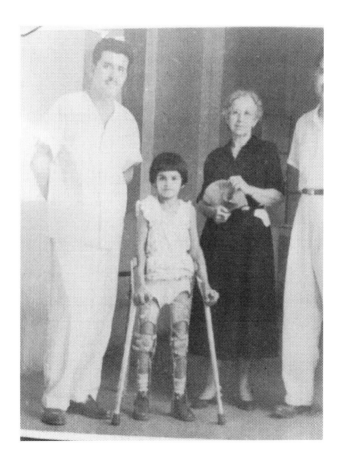

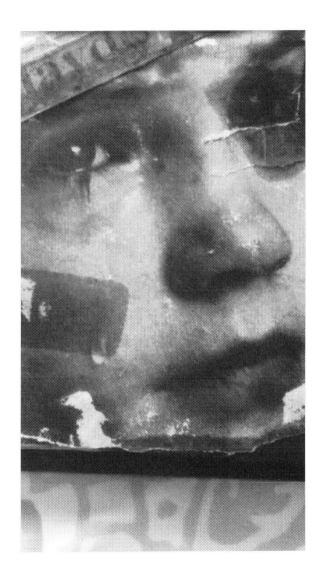

Chapter 2

Quinseyera

It is a Mexican tradition that when young girls turn fifteen years old she has a big party called a Quinseyera, a celebration that the girl has entered adulthood. The girl usually wears a white dress similar to a wedding dress, has a big cake, food, and presents from guests and family members. When I turned fifteen years old, I did not have a party or celebration. All my friends asked me if there was going to be a party, but neither my mother nor any family members made an effort to make it happen. I received no cake, party, or gifts, so I told myself if I ever have a girl, I will make sure she gets a Quinseyera. I paid my uncle, at the age of fifteen, to build three more rooms on the side of my house, which I transformed into a tortilla shop. One day I saw a tortilla machine maker for sale in the paper, and I bought it for seven hundred pesos. My uncle and I set it up in the shop and started making tortillas for sell by the dozen. I was loaned all the material to make the tortillas, the corn, the firewood, and everything to prepare my first batch. I learned how to operate the machinery and hired three older women to help me run the shop.

In one month, I sold all the tortillas that the first load of corn made. I paid what I owed for the loan of materials and bought another load of corn to keep the shop going. The business was excellent and started making real money with repeat customers that enjoyed the great taste and flavor of my homemade tortillas. In three years, I made forty thousand dollars from the tortilla shop. I also started selling charcoal from the leftover-burnt firewood that was used to boil the corn. Additionally, I started selling masa for tamales and soups, which is like a thick flat taco. I met many people while working at the shop. I felt good that I started my own business and that it was profitable. The extra money I made I supported the baby boy my mother left with me giving him everything a child needed; food, clothes, and toys.

My mother would visit once a week or possibly every two weeks; at times instead of visiting her children she would go dancing. She would buy herself expensive dresses and neglect her child, which was no surprise to me, so I took it upon myself to provide for her child. When I realized I had no real mother, I went to my birthplace, looking for my father and when I found him, I was very excited about it. A week after I was in the town, I saw my dad for the first time in my life. He ran to me picking me up from my wheelchair, crying as he gave me a big, strong hug. He was continually saying he was so sorry that he was unable to find and take care of me when I was little. He explained that my mother left him taking me with her to leave me with other family members instead of allowing him to raise me. My father said their marriage did not work because my mother always wanted to go out dancing with other men, and he said he was not going to dress the doll for others to play with her.

My father took me to his farm, and we stayed there a week. It was one of the best weeks of my life. He showed me kindness, love, compassion and was very proud of me for making it this far and becoming a beautiful girl. We talked about everything catching up with each other's lives. He took me everywhere and showed me fun and exciting places we enjoyed each other's company building a relationship between a father and daughter after a seventeen years separation. My dad gave me six gold bracelets and five thousand dollars to take and save. While I was there, I asked him if we could acquire my birth certificate because I never had it. We went to the town's city hall and registered for me to receive it. I finally had my birth certificate after so many years. It was time for me to get back home to my business. I told him I had to leave but would return the first chance I had. The entire side of his family gathered and gave me a great farewell. My father took me to the bus hugged and kissed me and sent me on my way. After a two day, bus ride I made it back home and the business was running well, and all the employees did a good job while I was out. When I arrived home, I showed my friends and family the gifts I received from my dad.

Three months after returning home from visiting my Dad, I received my passport to enter the United States of America. That was a good day in my life. Shortly after that, a woman, was interested in buying my tortilla shop, so I agreed to sell it for three thousand dollars. I took a short break to relax and enjoy life, but I was still watching my mother's son. I raised him until he was seven years old, taking him to school in the morning and pick him up in the afternoon. During the time, I was raising him I was also selling candy, fruit juice, ice cream, and charge the little children one peso to watch cartoons on the television. All the neighborhood children would come to buy treats and watch fun TV shows.

I was only able to go to the border between Mexico and the United States. I would go to the stores buy clothes, perfumes, makeup, and other American products and sell it in Mexico for a large profit. People would place special orders for individual items or products, and I would purchase and then sell it to them. I went to visit my dad again and took many American products to sell to my family members. During this trip, I met my whole family and had a great time. I traveled with my dad, and he showed me nice places, different farms and ranches in Mexico. I stayed three weeks and got to know my father and family better; they were all very friendly and kind to me. When I returned to my house, I was alone for a while because my mother had taken her son back across the border. I started having fun with my friends and going out to the city, towns, stores, movies, and parties. I never drank beer, got drunk, did drugs, nor hung around with bad people. I had a great time as a young adult woman. I made the most of life now that I was better physically and doing well financially. I always kept myself clean and dressed nice even though I did not have a boyfriend nor attracted to anyone. Many men liked me and pursued me, but none of them was my type. I could not see myself with them, so I denied the men who wanted me to be their girlfriend. I was nineteen years old by this time, and I was enjoying life, as I never had before. My whole life was ahead of me and I was ready to move forward and "ride life into a new chapter".

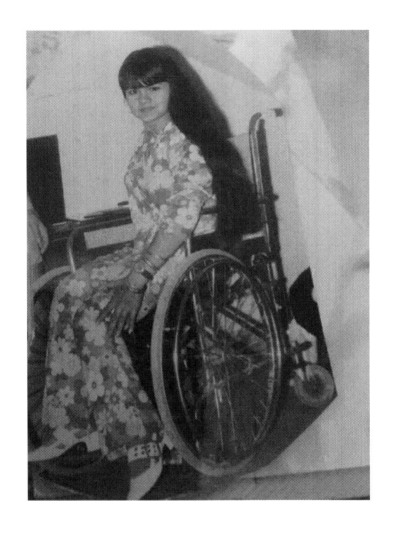

Chapter 3

First Kiss

I was twenty years old now when I met this handsome young man in Sinaloa, Mexico. I saw him for the first time at a cousin's house, and I fell in love with him at first site. He was a twenty-three years old young man who had the same feelings for me as I had for him. He was very kind to me, and we talked about everything, getting to know each other better. He was a college graduate with a bright future ahead of him. So after a couple of days of us talking and getting to know each other he asked me to be his girlfriend, and I accepted happily. We went to the movie theater, to eat ice cream, to the park and the fairgrounds with rides, shows, and games. We kissed the first time in the park in a gazebo covered with flowers and vines. He was my first true love and my first kiss.

We were together for two years when he asked me to marry him, and I said yes. I could not believe it; all my life people told me I was never going to have a man love me or want to marry me. Here I was, on the way to proving them wrong. We did not argue or fight. It felt great to have someone love me and to love. He went to ask my dad for my hand in marriage, and my father agreed because he knew he was a good man. When he went to ask my mother's permission to marry me, she asked him who his parents were. It turns out that we were blood-related, and that marriage was out of the question. I was so broken hearted I cried for months with unbelievable pain. We stopped all communication and went our separate ways.

I moved to San Luis, Arizona and worked at a furniture store for two years. I bought my first car, a 1958 Oldsmobile Classic and learned how to drive. My uncle Gilbert taught me to drive which only took me two weeks. I was driving one day, with my young brother, cruising around the town and a bus accidentally crashed into us. I suffered major injuries from the steering wheel, which plowed into my chest and shoulders leaving me with twelve stitches, bruised, battered, and hospitalized for one week. Fortunately, my brother received no injuries. After I had healed, I rode in taxies, everywhere because I was afraid of getting into another driving accident.

I was taking a taxi home one rainy day after work at the furniture store where I was sharing a taxi with another woman going in the same direction I was. The taxi driver dropped her off first and began acting very friendly and trying to get to know me. He then stopped to buy some soda pop and returned with two already opened with straws. He said, "I got you one" and gave it to me. I started to drink it trusting the man who was acting friendly. After I finished the drink I began to feel dizzy, sick, and nausea with my head spinning, I passed out. The taxi driver, I later found out, put a drug in my soda. I was a victim of a predator taking advantage of disabled young women. I woke in a hotel room beaten, bruised, bloody, and raped. The hotel's housekeeping found me and called the police and ambulance who took me to the hospital where I stayed for three days. Three months later the doctor notified me that I had become pregnant. He asked me if I wanted to keep or abort the child, I told the doctor I would keep the child.

My father received the news of what happened to me, and he arrived soon afterward. He asked me some questions about the taxi driver, and after he had the information, he went looking for him. My father located the driver he beat him, broke his nose, blackens both his eyes, and knocked out his teeth. When the police arrived, my dad told them what the taxi driver had done to me. The police knew of the report filed, identifying the man as the person that had assaulted me. The driver later was sentenced to a lot of time in prison. My mother showed up and attempted to convince me to abort the child, and I refused her advice. I had a healthy pregnancy with no complications with only two weeks of morning sickness and a good appetite. I craved fruits and vegetables and could not eat meat due to the smell of it made me ill. The doctors could not tell me if I was going to have a girl or a boy, but I believed I would be a better mother to my child than my mom ever was to me.

I took my passport and headed for the United States because I wanted to leave Mexico. I stopped in Yuma, to tell my mother I was going to live in the United States because I was no longer comfortable in Mexico. She asked me to stay there with her for a while, and I agreed. One morning I woke and started having pain and cramps in my stomach. I went to the bathroom, while sitting I felt a sharp pain, my water broke, and I the baby was coming. I got off the toilet, laid on the floor face down and I pushed when my baby started coming, delivering a healthy precious baby girl. I was all alone in the house because everyone was at work, so I cut the umbilical with my nails and wrapped my little girl in a towel. My brother arrived home from school, seeing me he went to tell a neighbor that I had given birth, and I needed a paramedic. The paramedics arrived, placed us both on the bed checking us both. The next day there was a story about me, in the local newspaper, a disabled woman giving birth alone on the bathroom floor, I saved the article. I wanted to name my daughter Alva Rocio, but my mother's husband asked if I could call her Rosie like his mother and I agreed. My first child was Rosie Navidad a beautiful baby girl who

I loved very much. I gave birth at 10:00 a.m. on the floor of my mother's trailer September 10, 1971. "The grandeur of my spirit was stronger than my incapacity."

Chapter 4

Second Chances

I decided to stay in the United States of America with my mother and give her an opportunity to redeem herself for the way she treated me when I was young. Things started well. My mother and her new husband bought a new three-bedroom trailer, and I got a room with a bathroom. My mother's husband would always get angry over my brother's mischievousness and began beating him. My mother helped me for a while until she started having problems with her husband. She would take her anger out on my brother and me. My mother would prepare her husband steak, potatoes, and salad and give my brother and me scrambled eggs; therefore, I started cooking for myself. One day I received a bank statement in the mail showing I had $45,000 in my bank account. My mother and her husband read the bank statement and said to give them the money to pay off the new trailer, promising to get me a green card, and that we would be a happy family. They took the money and bought a motorcycle, a white Volkswagen bug spending the money carelessly leaving me only seven hundred dollars. After spending the money, they started acting different, complaining about my baby and me. Meanwhile, I had my neighbor babysit my child and enrolled into adult school at Yuma High School. I learned how to speak clearer English and obtained a primary education. I had a great teacher who was patient and kind while teaching me. He made it easy for me to learn, and I graduated in three years. When I graduated, I could speak English fluently but out of the forty students, only ten of us graduated. We had a graduation ceremony where I received a high school diploma. I was happy, excited, and proud of my accomplishment. After graduation, I attended college at night, and I worked in the daytime.

I worked at several jobs, babysitting the neighbor's kid; I worked cutting people's hair, sewing, and ironing clothes. I also began working at a vegetable factory, packing dates, lettuce, broccoli, cauliflower, and other vegetation. I started saving money and opened a bank account with Valley National Bank. I graduated with fifteen thousand dollars and kept it a secret. I began to go out in the evenings with my best friend Carmen and other girlfriends, to shows, parties, and bars that played live Mexican and Country music. I liked American music more than Mexican music; it sounded better to me at that time. I was having a lot of fun with my friends. We had great laughs and enjoyable nights. One night my friend Carmen said, "I am taking you to a place that plays the best music."

I agreed to go and wore a long black dress with red high heel sandals and a red a flower in my hair. We went to a place called the Saddle Club. She pushed me in my wheelchair to a booth where she ordered a margarita for herself and a Coca Cola for me. The music was playing, and it was some of the greatest sounding Country music. My friend would dance with people; I never liked to get on the dance floor, so I stayed seated. I would just enjoy the atmosphere and the moment. Our other girlfriends showed up and sat at our booth laughing and having a great time. They were wild girls on the loose.

I noticed that the man playing the steel guitar was smiling at me and giving me the eye. I told my girlfriends "I bet you five dollars that the man from the band will come over to talk to me." They all bet and put the money at the center of the table waiting to see if it would happen. After the band had taken a short break, the band members left to get drinks and go the restroom. The man playing the steel guitar approached me saying "Hola, Como te yamas?" Which means ''Hi what's your name" and I said "Hayde." He said, "You know how to speak English?" I said, "Yes, what do you think just because I look Mexican I do not know how to speak English?" He smiled and said, "Well that is good." I asked his name, and he said, ''Sammy Lee Watson." He sat down and began chatting with me. We talked about various topics; he asked where I was from, how old I was, if I was single, what city I lived in, he asked lots questions. I asked him several questions some similar to what he asked me, others about his music and other essential questions to get to know him better. We learned a lot about each other that night. He asked me for my phone number, which I gave to him. He went back to the stage because the break was over and played more country music. I won the bet with my girlfriends keeping the fifteen dollars. They were surprised and excited for me except one who was jealous. It had gotten late, and my friends and I were leaving he said he was glad to meet me and that he would give me a call.

The next day at nine o'clock in the morning, I heard the phone ring. Answering it, I heard Sam say, "Hello is Hayde there," I said, "hi this is Hayde." We talked on the phone for a long while getting to know each other. We made plans for him to come over the next day and that I would cook a meal for us. I prepared what I considered a traditional Mexican lunch for us. When he arrived, I greeted him and invited him inside the house. My very good friend, Maria Rodriguez was with me that day, who later became the godmother of my first boy. Sam and I talked about many things concerning our lives. I told him that the food was ready and asked if he was ready to eat, he replied "yes." He sat at the table, and I served him. He enjoyed the meal I had prepared, complimenting me on the flavor of the food saying I was an excellent cook. Then he had to go rehearse with his band but we made another date meet the following day.

The next day he arrived by taxi with red roses, white flowers, and a box of chocolates for me. That day I introduced my daughter '' Rosie'' to him. My daughter said who are you and Sam replied, "I'm your dad", and she got excited saying she liked him. We all went out to eat Chinese food and had a fun day out in the city. When we returned home, Sam met my mother for the first time. She was very impressed with him and said she liked and approved of him instantly. They became acquainted with each other, and things were looking good for him with my mother, and brother. That evening we went to the drive-in theater, and while watching the movie, he leaned over and kissed me for the first time. Later that night when he took me home, he told me he would like to marry me. I was very surprised, happy, and excited, but I told him ''we will see.'' The next day he came again, and we went out into the city shopping for clothes. When we finished shopping and outside the store, he got on one knee, pulled out a ring, and said, "will you marry me," and I replied "yes." We hugged, kissed and later we went to see what was necessary to get married at the courthouse. We were advised to bring our birth certificates and set up an appointment to be married by a judge. The date they set for us was February 23, 1978. "Marriage is a new life between two people."

Chapter 5

A New Life

I started a new life with my new husband, who adopted my daughter, loved her as his own and she looked up to him as her father. My life changed with my dream of happiness, finally coming true, to have my life and family. A week later, we left for Sammy's home in Tennessee to have an extended honeymoon and to get to know his family. My daughter was in school, so she had to stay with my mother until school was out, and I had found a place for us to live. I felt horrible about leaving her and knew I was going to miss her very much. I told her I was leaving for a little while, but would be back very soon, she cried and said it would be okay.

We traveled on the Greyhound bus for three days from Arizona to Tennessee. I saw many places I had not seen before it was a fun adventure. The further away from my daughter I got, the more it hurt. I cried often, but my husband would always reassure me that we would go back soon to pick her up. It was raining, snowing, and freezing when we reached Nashville,

Tennessee. I was accustomed to the warm weather of the deserts, so the cold weather was quite chilling. We stayed at a hotel overnight waiting for his family members to pick us up the next day. My husband's sister Virginia and her husband Willy arrived and were very kind to me. We got along as soon as we met. They took us to Lebanon, Tennessee, to my new mother-in-law's home where the rest of the family was waiting and eating. The entire family was very friendly and hospitable. We all ate talked and had a great time getting to know each other. We stayed two weeks with his family. His family welcomed me warmly; being a Watson was very exciting.

My husband took me to all the nice places in Tennessee and showed me where he grew up and lived. He also took me to the Elvis Presley's house. We visited his entire family and his friends as well. I got along with everyone, and they all seemed to enjoy our conversations. After being there for two weeks, we left heading for Orlando, Florida to his brother's house staying there for two weeks. We enjoyed the beaches, had an impressive time, visiting all the nice places, and went site seeing in Florida. His brother enjoyed our company and was happy for us. After spending time with my new brother-in-law, we traveled to Green Bay, Wisconsin, and I learned I was pregnant. I was so happy and excited that I was going to have another baby. We stayed there for three weeks while my husband played his steel guitar in country music shows. While we were there, he made enough money to purchase a light green 1978 Buick station wagon and drove us around the city.

After our stay in Green Bay, we traveled to Chicago, Illinois and stayed there for several weeks while my husband and the band played many different locations. I had a lot of fun in Chicago; we drove around the city and ate great food. It was also a lot of fun at night at the bars and clubs watching my husband play country music and watching everyone dance. The other band members, their wives, and girlfriends were very kind to me. We were young, alive, and full of energy ready to take on the world; we were having a blast. We left Chicago, flew to New York and stayed for a week. My husband and his band had several shows to perform there, but we were still able to tour the city. We went to see the statue of liberty, which was a dream come true for me, to be there, seeing the Lady Liberty and enjoying my newfound freedom. I was very grateful to be in the United States, and to have come that far in my life. We visited many different places, eating various delicious foods, attended many different shows and concerts in New York. We had exciting times.

We traveled to many other places that were on the band's schedule of performances. My husband and the band also performed shows in Canada. I did not go to Canada with them because I was getting sick from the pregnancy and I did not have my passport with me. The doctor told me, I could no longer be on the road traveling, and I needed to stay home and rest. Following the doctor's orders, I took a plane to

Nashville while my husband toured in Canada for one month. While he was on tour, his family took excellent care of me making sure I always ate well and rested. The entire family was excited that a new baby was coming into the family. When my husband returned, we went to a casino in Kentucky where I won the bingo jackpot totaling $1,300! My husband and I had a lot of fun we were laughing with joy. Shortly after my bingo win, my husband received a call from a booking manager who heard my husband play the steel guitar. The manager was impressed with Sammy's playing, and he wanted him to play with Kenny Rogers, Freddy Fender, and several others who were performing and recording at a studio in North Hollywood, California. Therefore, we traveled to California staying there for a week while he recorded the steel guitar as background music for the Country Music artists. I liked California so much I decided I wanted to live there when we settle down. "I fell in love with California."

Chapter 6

My Children

My husband and I decided to stay in California and have our baby boy. We decided to name him Sammy Lee after my husband. We rented a house in Bell, California. I later called my mother and told her bring my daughter to live with me. When my daughter and I saw each other again, we were so happy and excited we both cried tears of joy. She was also pleased to see her father. We talked for days about what we did while we were apart I promised her I would never leave her again. We bonded mother and daughter developing a very special relationship. She was curious and asking why my stomach was big, that is when I told her she was going to have a baby brother, and she was very excited.

I gave birth at the Los Angeles County Harbor Medical Hospital in Torrance, California after twelve hours of very painful labor to a nine-pound twenty-two-inch baby boy, Sammy Lee Junior. They put my baby boy in an incubator for seven days after which I was able to hold and feed him. He got bigger and stronger each day until they finally said "Ok Hayde you are ready to be discharged". We returned to our home in Bell were we stayed for a year. We left for Oregon because my husband had the property he purchased when he was younger and wanted to sell it to buy a new and better place for us all. We stayed in Oregon a week while a man that wished to build a new home purchased the property. We used some of the money to buy a brand new car a 1979 Ford Mercury Cougar, new wheelchair for me, and steel guitar and speakers for when he performed with his band.

My husband was preparing to go on an extended tour, and I could not be on the road with my newborn baby and daughter. Therefore, we decided for the children and me to stay in San Luis Rio Colorado, Mexico. I stayed there, had apartments built on the property I owned, rented them out making enough money to support my children and me. I was pregnant again with another baby boy, and I decided to name him David Lee after one of my husband's band members because he was always nice to me and got along well with my husband. I enrolled my daughter in school in a small town by the border called Somerton, Arizona where I decided to stay until I was eight months pregnant. I moved to San Bernardino, California to give birth to my son because the doctors in Arizona did not want to deliver my baby because I was a high-risk pregnancy. On September 23, 1981, I gave birth to my third child at Saint Bernadine Medical Center.

After David Lee was born, I went back to Mexico and lived on my property until my second son was ready to go to Kindergarten.

Sammy learned to speak Spanish before speaking English. All my neighbors and tenants loved my kids, who looked like their American father and his family. Some people did not believe that they were mine because they looked nothing like me. My husband was on tour for three years, always on the road playing from one location to another. He finally had a break, and we moved back to San Bernardino, California because I liked the place when we visited it. It was a big valley surrounded by nice beautiful mountains and was close to everything. I enrolled my daughter in the sixth grade at Lincoln Elementary School and my son, Sammy, in Kindergarten. He only spoke Spanish, and it took him two years to learn how to speak and read English.

I met a man named Alfredo and he bought merchandise from the Salvation Army, Goodwill, and many thrift stores. He would wash the clothing, iron them making them look new and would sell them at the swap meet in different locations. He would sell me large loads of merchandise for a low price. I purchased a van, transported all this merchandise to Mexico selling it at for higher prices because the people loved American made products. I realized I could make a lot of money in this type of business. Therefore, I would purchase a large load for one hundred dollars and sold all of it in Mexico for six hundred dollars. I did this to make extra income since my husband had settled down and was no longer making money on tour. My husband got a local gig at a bar called the Silver Spur and was very close to home. I had continued this gypsy type work for many years before I burned out doing it. I also started selling merchandise at the local Swap Meet at the Orange Show Fair Grounds. I managed to save enough money to move my family and me out of the neighborhood we lived in which had lots of gang activity; I did not want my kids to grow up in that environment. We moved to a nicer neighborhood close to the mountains in the Foothills area, which was a good choice; my sons got involved in sports and not gangs. My daughter found a boyfriend, later married him, and had two children, a boy named German and a girl named Vada. They moved out on their own living in the same neighborhood as us keeping in touch daily. I also helped her by watching her kids while she went to work. Although my younger son was diagnosed with a heart murmur, my kids grew up safe and healthy with no problems. "Children are God's Gifts."

CHAPTER 7

Separation

My husband and I started to argue and have marital complications. He would get drunk and verbally abuse everyone around him. I was terrified of a separation because I did not want my kids to grow up without a dad, but it was not working out between us. I did not wish to have my children blame me later for our separation, they were young and did not understand what was going on. One day my husband said, "I'm leaving" and he took off to Tennessee and left two young kids and me, one was eleven and the other eight years old. He did not tell the eleven-year-old boy, Sammy Jr., he was leaving. He came in the house after playing with his friends and discovered that his dad had left him for good. It was a hard time for the whole family, but we had to be strong and believe that we were going to be all right.

I felt very sad watching my kids grow up without a dad when they needed him the most. My oldest son joined a baseball team to get his mind off the loss of his father, who he loved and missed very much. I did my best to raise my boys the right way they always had good grades, they graduated from high school, and never arrested for any crimes. Sometime after that, my daughter divorced her first husband; it did not work out between them either. She found out late that she was not ready for marriage, but both parents remained longtime friends and shared custody without court involvement. They remained supportive of each other, helping any time one or the other needed assistance with anything. I did my best to help them by watching their children while they worked or went out for recreational activities. "Separation affects everyone."

CHAPTER 8

Celebration

My life has turned out to be a celebration, after many years all my kids grew up and had children of their own. We gather for holidays, birthday, celebrating life as a family enjoying each other's company with excellent food and many gifts. We get together any chance we can, talking having family conversations, and prayer. I feel like the mission God sent me on, is completed disability and all. "Celebrate life because it's a miracle of grand proportion."

The End

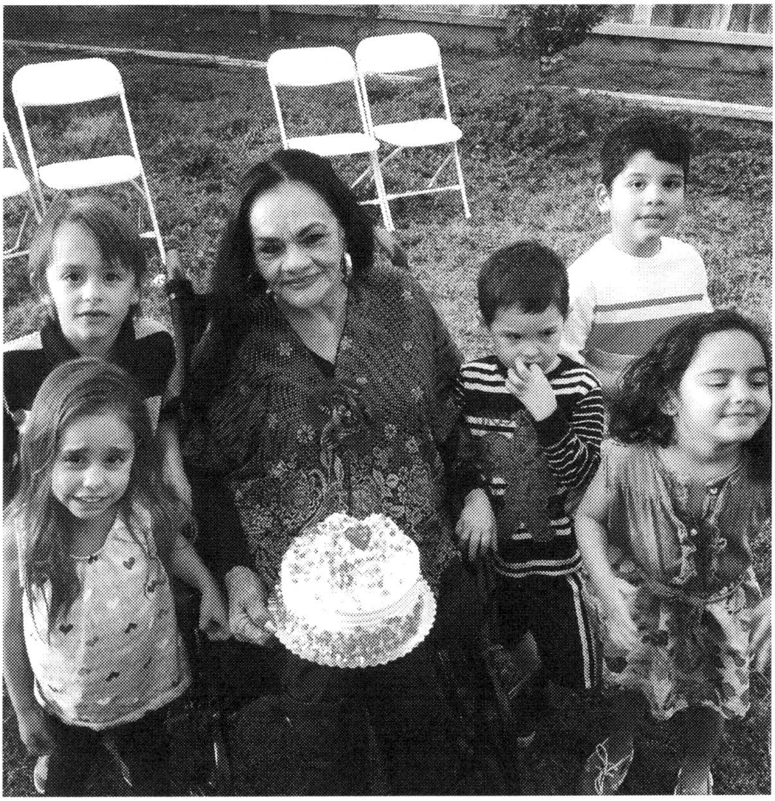

Printed in the United States
By Bookmasters